very small
LIVING
SPACES

Design and Decorating Strategies
to Make the Most of What You Have

BY BETH FRANKS

COLUMBUS
BOOKS

A FRIEDMAN GROUP BOOK

Copyright © 1989 by Michael Friedman Publishing Group, Inc.

First published in Great Britain in 1989
by Columbus Books Limited
19–23 Ludgate Hill
London EC4M 7PD

British Library Cataloguing in Publication Data
Franks, Beth
  Living Spaces.
    1. Small residences. Interior design
    I. Title
  747

ISBN 0-86287-433-5

VERY SMALL LIVING SPACES
was prepared and produced by
Michael Friedman Publishing Group, Inc.
15 West 26th Street
New York, New York 10010

Editor: Tim Frew
Designer: Marcena Mulford
Art Director: Mary Moriarty
Photo Editor: Christopher Bain
Production Manager: Karen L. Greenberg

Typeset by BPE Graphics, Inc.
Color separations by Hong Kong Scanner Craft Co Ltd.
Printed and bound in Hong Kong by Leefung-Asco Printers, Ltd.

Dedication

To my parents, Jean and Jerry, and sisters, Katie and Sue, who taught me how to maintain a balance between too many possessions and not enough space, one secret of living happily in a small home.

Acknowledgements

I'd like to thank Kathleen Poer, of Spacial Design in San Francisco, and DAK, of Koch Landmark Developments in Cincinnati, for sharing their design expertise. Thanks also to Judith Miley, of Clairson International, for research leads, and to the many manufacturers who provided product literature and photographs. Special thanks to my editor, Tim Frew, for trimming verbiage and straightening out structural problems in the manuscript, and to Marcy Mulford, for her help with the captions. Finally, I'm grateful for my friends, Maya, Sara, and Matt, who provided entertainment and emotional support throughout the writing process.

CONTENTS

INTRODUCTION
page 8

INTRODUCTION

I f you live in an apartment, condominium, or small house you probably feel squeezed for space. Since many of yesterday's mid-size apartments have been divided into today's efficiencies, more and more people have had to make do with small, oddly-shaped living spaces. The L-shaped apartment that has no walls to separate the sleeping area and the kitchen, the space with high ceilings and an irregular floor, the one-bedroom in a converted factory that has no entrance foyer and a sink and shower in the living area—all of these examples create perplexing design dilemmas.

VERY SMALL LIVING SPACES will help you find creative solutions to your design problems. Chapter One guides you through the planning stages: deciding on space priorities, determining the amount of usable space you have, and drawing up a workable floor plan. There are also strategies for making a space seem larger, and advice on coordinating elements such as color, texture, and scale.

Chapter Two explores the many options for structuring a small space, for all kinds of uses. You'll discover that a space can often serve dual-purposes: a closet may open up into a playroom for a child, a dining table may fold into a desk, and a platform or loft can serve as both a sleeping and lounging area. Chapter Three takes a look at ten case studies—people who've created exemplary environments structured to suit their individual living and working needs. Finally, at the end of the book, there is a comprehensive list of sources—manufacturers, retailers, and organizations that feature products or services of special interest to the small-space dweller.

Today's lifestyles encourage mobility, independence, and flexibility, and living spaces reflect this. No one book can supply all the answers, but with the ideas in VERY SMALL LIVING SPACES, you can design an environment that's efficient, beautiful, and tailored to your own needs. With thorough planning and a little ingenuity, living in a small space can be a very comfortable experience.

Chapter One

PLANNING AND ASSESSING LIVING NEEDS

E. Allen McGee/FPG Irtl.

More and more people are opting to live in small homes or apartments because of economics or location. Yet trying to fit all your living needs into a limited area with taste and style is no easy task, even for the design-conscious decorator. Certain universal necessities—dining, sleeping, bathing, storage, seating, entertaining—must have their place, but trying to fit them all into a studio apartment can create a chaotic, claustrophobic atmosphere.

Organizing a small space has a lot to do with creating an illusion of more rather than less. Finding every last inch of space in a small home or apartment and using it efficiently and comfortably is the crux of this organization. Throughout this book, we'll be looking at ways to create affordable and accessible, yet luxurious living spaces.

The first step is to take a good hard look at what you've got to live with. Think about how you want your living space to function: Are you a weekend parent who needs a place for the kids to stay? Do you entertain? Do you work out with weights at home? Once you've assessed your needs, it is much easier to devise imaginative solutions to transform your small space into a completely functional and beautiful dream home.

Form Follows Function

Before you draw up a plan and start rearranging furniture—or walls—on paper, it's important to decide on your space priorities. Often, rooms are used for more than one activity, so you need to decide which function is most important. For instance, assume you have the luxury of a spare bedroom. You like having it available to use as a guest room, but you also want to set up a home office where you can write the great American novel at night and on weekends. Since you have guests only once or twice a year, it makes sense to make the room primarily an office, with a daybed, Murphy bed, or some other "disguised" treatment for the secondary function of guest room. On the other hand, if you often have guests from out of town, but have only one bedroom, you might want to designate "guest room" as the living room's primary function. Deep banquette seating converts to a single bed in nothing flat, as do some futon frames. There are also ottomans designed to open up into beds. For a double bed "couch," use a futon frame, or try the classic solution, a sofa bed.

This room's primary function is dining, and it even features two options: a table and a countertop breakfast area. Yet it gracefully incorporates a living area that adapts to both sitting and sleeping, thanks to the deep banquettes.

© Derrick & Love 1987

R. Abraham/FPG Intl.

This kitchen is a model of cleverly utilized space. Cabinets go almost all the way to the ceiling, and the cantilevered counter serves triple duty for food preparation, dining, and storage. The work island incorporates a sink and allows several people to work in the kitchen without stepping on each other's toes.

Living and dining are frequent cohabitors—a large plant and a strategically placed chair are all that separate this dining area from the living room. Placing a table on the diagonal helps make a small room seem larger by breaking up the space in an unexpected way.

Maybe you have a small kitchen that also features a dining area. If you love to cook, but hate the lack of counter space, consider remodeling the kitchen to include more cabinets and a cantilevered counter that can also be used for dining. Or you might decide to sacrifice the secondary function of eating in the kitchen to make it a more efficient work area. Or perhaps you love to give large, sit-down dinner parties, but lack a formal dining room. It may be possible to create an elegant dining space in your living room, using a combination of collapsible tables and coffee tables that can be raised to dining height.

If you live in a studio apartment, you need to define the main activity areas and create zones within the one room. In a large studio, standing screens, wall units, and even pull-down shades can be used to divide space. Decide which basic activities to combine—sleeping/sitting, cooking/eating, eating/entertaining, or sitting/entertaining. Some activities don't naturally seem to go together, but can still be successful collaborators. For instance, an artist may use a 3-by-14½ foot (.9-by-4.4 meter) table for working, eating, displaying artwork or books, and even sleeping (with a mat). Underneath the table is extra space for books and storage. Obviously only you can decide what is really important to you. The most important point is to think about how you use your

Living and sleeping are another natural combination provided the "bed" is at least partially disguised. A hammock can be used for everyday lounging as well as for occasional overnight guests.

available space. List your main preferences, then brainstorm possibilities as to how to adapt your home to fit.

As you think about all the uses that a room has to perform, also consider how often it's used for each. If the uses are fairly concurrent (you sleep in the living room, for instance), you need a flexible setup, something that's easily transformed. Also think about what furnishings, accessories, and artwork you have, and what you want to keep in each room. You'll probably find that

you want to get rid of some stuff, and that there are other things you'd like to buy.

Consider your habits too. Do you want a room to accommodate your habits or change them? For instance, if you have perpetual piles of papers on the floor—ongoing projects and a sort of "visual" filing system— you must first decide whether you want to eliminate those piles, get them out of sight, or keep them in the open for easier access. The options are as simple as a file cabinet or cupboard for closed storage, and

open shelving, a table, or desk top for accessibility.

Finally, think about the emotional effect of the room. How would you like to feel when you're occupying this particular space? For instance, if you wake up and exercise in a room, you may want to fill it with warm colors (reds, oranges); whereas, if you use a room to unwind after work, cool colors (blues, greens) might be better. (See page 28 for more on the use of color.)

You are the architect of your destiny when it comes to your home—you can create an environment that's uniquely yours. And in searching for viable treatments of problem spaces, you may be surprised at what you come up with—sometimes the simplest solutions are right under your nose.

Left: Studio apartments call for imaginative, flexible use of space—everything must work together to create a harmonious effect. This apartment uses the three central support beams as natural dividers while unifying the separate areas with color and artwork. *Facing page*: This is the same apartment viewed from the opposite end. Decorating tricks are essential in studios. White walls make the space seem to expand while the brown beams pull the eye upward, enhancing the height of the room.

Designer: Roberta Pincus/Photos (2): Bill Rothschild

Does It Measure Up?

Once you have a general idea of how you want your space to function, you need to find out exactly how much floor you are working with. Using a coil spring tape measure to insure accuracy, measure the length, width, and height of all the rooms, taking into account doors and windows, as well as protrusions such as radiators and elaborate moldings. Note any architectural features as well: fireplaces, alcoves, arched openings, built-ins, sliding or folding doors.

Also measure the closets. Most likely a lot of wasted space is lurking in there that you'll eventually want to exploit. If you want to be really thorough, make note of all electrical outlets, light switches, and telephones. While you're at it, pay attention to available wall space. A wall unit, high shelves, or cupboards to the ceiling may be just what you need to expand available floor space: With minor construction, kitchen soffits can be removed for additional storage space, or the space between wall studs can be knocked out to create shallow shelves or cupboards.

Write your measurements in feet and inches, rather than inches alone, to avoid errors. (Does not pertain to the metric

Above: When measuring your space, take architectural features into account and think of ways to use them to best advantage. A shallow alcove is the focal point of this room thanks to a couch that fits snuggly inside. The alcove also acts as a large "frame" for the artwork.

Left: Use wall space for everything it's worth. This wall unit exploits the entire wall, from floor to ceiling, for housing storage, an entertainment center, and a workspace.

© Phillip H. Ennis

Above: Placing a large plant in the corner of a room and then shining a light up through its leaves will make the corner seem to disappear as well as create interesting patterns on the ceiling and walls.

Facing page: A few large pieces of furniture are actually better than smaller scale furnishings in a small space. This bulky sofa, placed against the wall, makes the room look longer; the rug also promotes this illusion.

system.) These dimensions will be the "blueprint" that enables you to play with the space without making expensive mistakes. When working with a plan, you may see immediately if the room is out of balance. You can play with the pieces you already own, as well as things you'd like to add, and you can figure out the best bets for remodeling or structural alteration.

Using these measurements, draw up a plan, to scale, of your existing space. Use graph paper that's divided into ¼-inch (6 millimeter) squares. Using a scale of ¼ inch to a foot, draw the outlines of the space in dark pencil or pen, leaving spaces for windows, doors, and protrusions. Any special features, such as built-in bookshelves or projecting columns, should be carefully drawn to scale. Then make symbols for your existing furniture, as well as any pieces you would like to buy. These don't have to be the exact shape as the real thing, but should be as close to scale as possible. (Yes, this means you'll need to measure the furniture too.) Cut out the furniture templates from light cardboard or heavy paper so you can move them around on the plan to find the best arrangement. Another method is to use onionskin or tracing paper as an overlay, sketching in various arrangements. Draw freehand until you settle on the final plan, then use a ruler to render the shapes more precisely. Likewise, if you opt for cardboard templates, once you finalize the floor plan, trace around the symbols to record the layout.

When arranging furniture, start with the most important piece. Separate large pieces so the room doesn't become unbalanced. In a very small room it's usually best to position large or bulky furniture—large sofas, heavy wood pieces, armoires, etc.—against a wall. Placing them in the middle of the room makes the furniture look bigger and the room smaller. Consider natural traffic patterns, and allow at least forty inches (one meter) for major pathways. If possible, arrange seating in a way that allows traffic to move around the grouping, not through it. A U-shape is one of the best ar-

Designer: Denise Balassi Assoc. Photo: Bill Rothschild

rangements to seat a lot of people in a small space.

The plan will show how much furniture can be included in one room, and where. But don't settle on the first arrangement that comes to mind. Since you don't have to drag real furniture around the room, brainstorm many options. Also, experiment with new furniture on paper: How would a wall unit work to divide the living and dining areas? Would a modular banquette solve your seating problems, or create a crowded feeling? Is there room for a rolling work island in the kitchen? Once you finalize your decisions, your plan will act as a buying guide.

It may also be possible to vary the existing layout of a home without making major structural alterations. For instance, you could construct a raised platform with a pull-out bed, on casters, underneath. Or if you have high ceilings, it may be possible to construct a loft without attaching it to the walls. Bolted and screwed together, it can be disassembled and taken with you when you move. Use your plan to explore the possibilities—built-in storage, an office/closet, a bed on pulleys that lowers from the ceiling, a fold-down table, a sleeping loft, whatever. Then work with a designer or carpenter to make sure your great ideas are viable.

While you should finish reading this book before settling on a final arrangement, it is good to start planning right away. Study what you like in these pages and in magazines, showrooms, and the homes of your friends. Look at what works—and what doesn't. Also pay attention to what attracts you: furnishings, fabrics, color, texture, or some ''special touch.'' All of these elements are important in creating a jewel of a small space.

Finally, photocopy your plan and carry it and a tape measure with you at all times. That way if you're out shopping and you unexpectedly come across the couch of your dreams on sale, you'll know by its measurements whether it's really perfect after all.

Photographs (2): © Derrick & Love 1987

Above: This vanity was squeezed into a small corner that previously went to waste. The glass block window provides natural light and privacy, making it an ideal spot to apply makeup.

Left: This studio apartment effectively combines living and sleeping areas. The wall of cupboards above the bed guarantees that incidentals are kept out of sight. Mirrors help to visually expand the space.

The Bottom Line

How much can you afford to spend? Again, budgeting is a matter of priorities. First you need to know what you want, then you decide what you can afford, and what's most important to purchase first. The least expensive approach is to decorate around your limitations. There are many design tech-niques and organizational products that will make a small space beautifully efficient. Sometimes a single piece of furniture can streamline your life dramatically. For instance, I revolutionized my life as a free-lancer by buying a convertible futon frame. For the five years I'd worked on staff for a pub-lisher, my desk had always been in the living room, but once I started editing out of my one bedroom apartment, I found my life was engulfed by work. The only time I could escape was when I slept! I solved the problem by moving my office into the "bedroom." My futon now functions as a couch by day, a bed by night. Three hundred dollars (four hundred Canadian dollars) for the frame was a small price to pay, considering the additional living and working space.

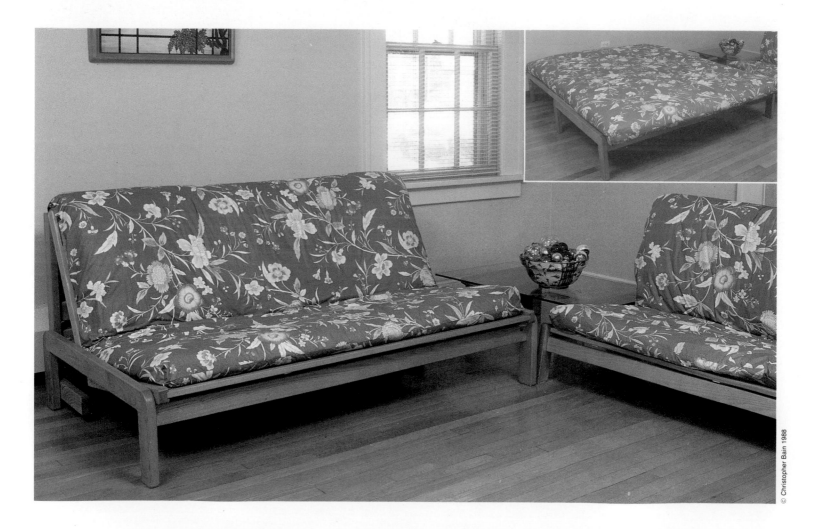

Courtesy Intl. Contract Furnishings Inc.

A good rule of thumb is provided by designer Arnold Friedmann, in COMMONSENSE DESIGN: ''...in order to create good interior design two things are important: to know when to stop and to do at least one thing well.'' Doing one thing well may mean that a sizeable chunk of your budget goes for one piece, but if it pulls a room together and solves problems at the same time, it may be well worth the expense.

Before making a major purchase, look at the various styles, makes, and price ranges that are available. Investigate specialty and department stores that stock fine furniture, antique shops, discount and secondhand stores. Do a lot of comparison shopping, and carry a tape measure and a

Above: Nesting tables are out of the way on a daily basis, but can be a lifesaver if you like to entertain. They are available in a wide variety of styles—from early American charm to Italian designer chic.

Facing page: A convertible futon frame flips from a couch to a bed in the blink of an eye. They're great for studio apartment dwellers as well as for those who lack a guest room.

small notebook with you to record measurements and prices. Window shopping can be very educational—you'll soon learn to recognize what constitutes quality in any given piece. Avoid fads, unless you plan to redecorate again next year, and be careful of buying on impulse. Not only will you avoid mistakes, but things do go on sale periodically.

Ready-to-assemble (or knockdown) furniture can save money as well as space. Most ready-to-assembles are imported from Scandinavia or Germany, and dealers say that being able to ship and store it unassembled represents a savings to both the store and the customer. Because it's often modular you can buy various pieces at different times and know that they'll work together. Best of all, just about everything imaginable is available as knockdown: platform beds with built-in nightstands as well as headboard and underbed storage; component wall units, entertainment centers, and bookcases; computer desks and office equipment with optional typing returns, file drawers, and lap desks; kids' bunk beds, trundle beds, and work stations; and dining room and kitchen tables with self-storing leaves.

If you're handy, you may want to build in some changes to your apartment without al-

Taps Loft Inc.

tering the original structure. Though your labor will be free, materials must be included in your budget. Most people call a professional when doing major alterations. This is obviously going to cost money. If you plan to tear down walls, to completely reshape the space from the ground up, talk to an interior designer or architect before proceeding. This too,

can be expensive. A small room change might cost anywhere from fifty to two thousand dollars (sixty to three thousand Canadian dollars), while a major overhaul could run from two thousand to thirty thousand dollars (three thousand to thirty-seven thousand Canadian dollars) per room.

To find a good architect or interior designer, check with local and national professional organizations (American Institute of Architects, the American Society of Interior Designers, Interior Designers of Canada), ask your friends, visit the designer showcases held in your area, and check the Yellow Pages. Pay attention to good design in business establishments, restaurants, and private residences, and ask who did the work. You may also find designers featured in local publications. Interview and get bids from several designers before committing to one.

Make a shopping list of everything you want, including any outside help from professionals, then prioritize according to needs, desires, and expense. Usually it's a good idea to solve your alteration problems first, but sometimes you need to compromise. For instance, you may want to completely rearrange the kitchen walls and ceiling, but after talking to a couple of designers, and discovering that it would cost twice as much as you had thought, you may decide to upgrade your living area first.

If you have plenty of great ideas but lack funds, be on the lookout for bargains and don't overlook "cheap chic" outlets such as the Salvation Army, thrift stores, unfinished furniture stores, hardware stores, and restaurant supply outlets. You may also be comforted by decorator Joan Bingham's words: "Good taste isn't for sale, expensive poor taste abounds in the apartments of those who lack imagination." It may take a while to bring your plan to reality, but by knowing what you want and working toward it, you'll be way ahead of those people with more money than sense.

E. Allen McGee/FPG Intl.

Left: Removing a wall nearly tripled available living space and opened up the room psychologically, as well. *Facing page*: Ready-to-assemble units come in all configurations, and are designed with the small-space dweller in mind.

Less Than Meets The Eye

Designers have many strategies to make a space look larger, but perhaps the easiest and most effective is the use of color. The colors of walls, ceilings, floors, drapes, furniture, and upholstery can have a great effect on the perception of the space as a whole.

Warm colors (red, orange) "advance" and make a room seem smaller, more intimate. Cool colors (blue, green) make walls recede, so the space seems larger. Intense hues, both warm and cool, create a confined feeling in a small space. As a general rule, save intense colors for the bathroom walls or a hallway to prevent their drama from overwhelming you. Also, if you rent, most leases stipulate "no dark colors," so before you move you'll have to repaint with white or a pastel to cover.

Perhaps because living spaces have been steadily shrinking in the past few years, white or off-white has become the modern classic wall color. White reflects light and seems to make the walls expand. White rooms appear spacious, provide unlimited options for color schemes, allow a scheme to be easily changed, and reflect lighting to create a brighter atmosphere. Paintings and artwork are emphasized when placed against white walls.

The most basic way of making space appear larger is to let the eye roam. One of the best ways to accomplish this is through a monocromatic color scheme (discussed in more detail later in the chapter). By painting utility pipes and other protrusions the same color as the surrounding areas they tend to blend in rather than stand out. This lack of contrast allows the eye to wander uninterrupted, making the room appear larger.

Volumes have been written on the psychological effects of

Chas Schneider/FPG Intl.

As seen at Boulder Ridge/Photo: Bill Rothschild

Above: White walls reflect light and make any room seem larger. White is especially effective in this under-the-roof space that could easily feel claustrophobic if painted with an intense color.

Facing page: A subtle pastel color scheme creates an open feeling in this small dining area. The glass tabletop and clean-lined chairs also promote an airy look, fostering the illusion of space.

color. For a sense of airiness and space, pale and pastel shades are best. On the other hand, sometimes rules are made to be broken. Vivid tones generally reduce spaciousness. At night, very dark, cool hues can make the walls seem to fall away. If you have your heart set on a midnight blue bedroom, you probably won't be satisfied until you've tried it, and it may end up being a dream come true. You're the best judge of what you can live with on a daily basis.

When choosing paint colors, remember that they look lighter on those little chips than they will on your walls. Yellow is especially deceiving. What looks like a pale pastel on the swatch may be maddeningly bright on the wall. To be really sure of what you're getting into, purchase a small quantity of the paints you're considering and try them in the room to be painted. Check light reflections from all sources at various times of day and night. Reflections of the red house across the street or seasonal changes in foliage can affect how gray paint looks on a wall. Have the paint salesperson lighten or darken the sample until you have found the perfect hue.

If hiring professionals, look for painters who tint their own paints. Although painting is something we often tackle our-

The light walls, natural lighting, and delicately patterned upholstery combine to create an open, airy feeling in this converted attic space. By placing large pieces of furniture in the center of the room, the space will appear larger.

selves, professionals can prevent a lot of headaches. They conscientiously prepare the surface, strike clean lines, make a minimal mess, and clean up afterwards. What at first seems an extravagance may end up being a net gain.

If you prefer the visual interest of wall coverings, papering one or two walls of a small room can make it look larger. Wall coverings with quiet, simple patterns also create an open, airy impression, whereas tight, complex patterns usually shrink a room. Some designers feel that using one pattern throughout the room—walls, ceilings, draperies, and upholstery—makes a room seem large because the eye isn't stopped by contrasts.

Stripes can trick the eye in some useful ways. For instance, in a small high-ceilinged room that feels like an elevator shaft, or in short hallways, horizontal stripes will make the walls look longer. In a room with a low ceiling, they are the most effective illusion-maker, making the ceiling appear higher, and in long, narrow rooms, they help shorten what may seem like interminable walls.

Metallic wall coverings expand space and make the corners of the room seem to disappear. Use caution, however, when hanging metallics, because even small flaws and protrusions in the walls will be emphasized. Wall preparation is important for all wall coverings, but it is crucial with metallics—be sure the surface is absolutely smooth and clean. If the whole-room approach is too glitzy, metallics should be used only on the ceiling to "lift off" the top of the room and to reflect light.

Mirrors create the ultimate optical illusion. A mirrored wall seems to double the space in a room, just as a half round table placed against it will appear to be a full circle. A wall of mirror-fronted cupboards will expand your storage space as well as create the impression of a more spacious room. And you can really go wild with mirrors in small enclosed spaces such as bathrooms and hallways; since the effect won't be overwhelming. In living, sleeping, and dining areas, place mirrors to reflect artwork, decorative objects, or furniture—obviously if there's nothing to reflect, the effect is lost.

For the same reason, be cautious when hanging mirrors, especially whole wall sections. A beautiful room or hallway can be ruined by the reflection of a heating duct, storage closet, fire escape, or toilet. Have a partner hold a mirror at every height and angle where you think you'd like to hang or install mirrors, and check to see what is reflected from every part of the room, both sitting and standing. Be on the lookout for architectural eyesores, and also be aware of what part of your life you may be reflecting for the neighborhood to see.

A *trompe l'oeil* mural or landscape can be used in a windowless small room to lead the eye out and beyond, and help create an added sense of depth and drama. Supergraphics and photo walls also create the illusion of depth and dimension, which makes a room seem larger than it is, but both have a tendency to overpower a room and may quickly become tiresome. A more moderate approach is to use wall space for pictures and shelves which help lead the eye upward, expanding living areas with vertical interest. A stenciled border also attracts the eye and makes a room appear larger.

A light-colored floor, whether carpet, vinyl, ceramic tile, marble, or painted wood, is ideal for stretching space. Polished wooden floors left bare also make the room seem larger. As a general rule, area rugs stop the eye and thus shrink space, but can be very useful for defining ''zones'' in a studio apartment.

Light fabrics also help promote the illusion of space. Cotton, muslin, Belgian linen, smooth silks and satins, voile, and organdy create a sense of airiness, especially in white or pale solid colors. Fabrics with a very small or open pattern are also effective. Stripes and ticking will trick the eye on upholstered furniture, just as they will in wall coverings, creating illusions of height or length.

Window treatments can also create spatial illusions. Tailored shades, shoji screens, shutters, vertical blinds, and even simple floor-length drapes emphasize spaciousness because they don't intrude visually on a room. To make windows appear larger, hang drapes beyond either side of the window, overlapping them slightly at the edge of the glass, so it looks like the window extends past the window frame. Floor-

Two views of one room in a small house (*facing page*). Colors, fabrics, and wall treatment work well together. Mirrors and glass block serve to visually enlarge the space.

Designers: Frec Kentop & Linda Malkin, K-Designs As seen at Designers Showcase · Photographs (3): Bill Rothschild

Living and dining areas balance each other nicely in this room. While furniture placement clearly defines the separate areas, the floorplan is open, permitting an easy flow from one activity to the other. Large round mirrors increase the feeling of space.

length blinds (ricepaper, matchstick, or venetian) extend the window to the floor.

For overall lighting that makes a small space seem larger, arrange fixtures so that light reflects off the ceiling and/or into the corners of the room. Small accent lights placed in the corners and directed upward through plants will create foliage patterns on the ceiling. You'll feel like you're sitting under a tree, and the corners and ceiling of the room will disappear. (Just be sure to position the lights so they won't burn the plants.) Track lighting and low-wattage spotlights can be used to define an area or to emphasize the separation between areas. You'll also need light for specific uses such as reading in bed, working at a desk, or highlighting a piece of art. Check design-conscious lighting stores for special lamps for small spaces.

Too much furniture in a small room creates a crowded effect, especially if it's small furniture. Strangely enough, a couple of large pieces in a simplified grouping are actually better— their exaggerated scale makes the space seem more expansive. Otherwise, look for pieces that are light in scale rather than small in size. Furniture that is light in color seems less massive than pieces with a dark finish. Wicker, rattan,

E. Allen McGee/FPG Intl.

These bi-fold doors trick the eye in two ways. Running from floor to ceiling they pull the eye upward and make the room seem taller. Running the width of the room and around the corner they also lead the eye horizontally. Both horizontal and vertical movements are reinforced by the slats in the doors.

bamboo, and ''see-through'' pieces of glass or lucite have a floating, airy quality and appear to take up less space.

As for upholstery, the larger the fabric pattern, the larger the furniture will appear. Large patterns, whether in the upholstery, wall coverings, or draperies, tend to draw focus in the room. To be safe, stick to small

patterns or solids in a small room, but again, don't be afraid to follow your instincts. If possible, before investing in fabric, arrange for an at-home demonstration, or buy a sample and drape it on the object for which it is intended. Does it look the same as it did in the store? Is the pattern too overpowering? Does it go with

your overall design scheme? Obviously multifunctional furniture adds to the versatility of a small space. This is no illusion, but a real advantage when living in a small apartment or home. Beds are, perhaps, the most common examples; however, there is a variety of commercially available furniture with built-in storage. You can also have pieces custom-made. For instance, Bay-area designer Kathleen Poer, owner of Spacial Design, created a file cabinet that doubles as a coffee table or a bench.

Modular units offer an endless number of possible arrangements. Since they are sold separately, you can tailor them to your specific needs. Extend a unit all the way to a door or entryway to make the room seem larger. Banquette seating exaggerates the length of the wall against which it's placed. A long banquette at dining height can serve as many as four purposes: lounging, eating at the table, sleeping, and storage (remove cushions to find lift-up lids). Multipurpose modular furniture can solve a lot of problems in tight spots. Wall units featuring built-in beds, tables, drop-leaf desks, shelves, and storage cabinets use vertical space that's otherwise wasted while yielding precious floor space.

Studio apartment dwellers need to be particularly inventive, since everything is happening in that one room. The best visual trick is to create a "free zone," leaving some part of the room open to create the impression of roominess. This zone can also be used for special activities such as hobby projects or entertaining.

Keeping things neat will help make your space seem larger by creating less distraction. Use storage units to hide incidental clutter: ashtrays, guest pillows and bedding, luggage, and special-use tableware. If you can also hide the functional things—TV, stereo, etc.—the room will tend to look bigger, since it's less crowded.

Facing page: This multifunctional wall unit features everything but the kitchen sink and also serves as a room divider.

Below: A built-in wall unit transforms this bedroom into a tidy hideaway with a luxurious home entertainment system.

More Than Meets The Eye

Coordinating design elements in tiny spaces is a big job. Color, texture, and scale all combine to create an overall impression. Visual tricks notwithstanding, it is important for all of the elements of a room to work together in order to be successful.

Colors are most effective when used monochromatically. When a color is repeated throughout its gradations, all areas of space and furnishings flow into each other and create a sense of expansiveness. But sometimes this works better in theory than in practice. For instance, the ultimate expansive treatment would be an all-white room. White on white creates a floating-in-space effect, but is hard to keep clean and can get boring. This scheme works if it's balanced with vivid accents in artwork, plants, pillows, and other accessories. White upholstery and carpet must be treated with a fabric guard or stain repellent, and every little bit of dirt is going to show. Be prepared to spend more time cleaning if you opt for white furnishings. If you have children or pets, be extra careful when selecting materials.

When planning a monochromatic scheme, be sure to choose a color that won't overpower the room, and one that won't bore you in a week. Neutrals—black, white, and beige—can be added without interfering with the basic colors. Though not strictly monochromatic, sometimes small dashes of another color can be successfully added.

Texture plays an important part in every interior. Combine dissimilar textures that are nonetheless compatible with one another, such as ''soft'' wools, leathers, and weaving set off against ''hard'' wood and glass. Let taste be your guide here, but strive to maintain a balance of textures throughout the space.

Scale is the size relationship of things to one another—the relative dimensions of spaces or objects. Furnishings must relate to the space as a whole —a grand piano in an 8-by-10 foot (2.4-by-3-meter) room may seem out of place. Furniture should also be balanced in scale and height to avoid an unsettling ''big city skyline'' look. Scale relates to human dimensions as well—a very deep sofa or exquisitely delicate dining room chairs may actually be out of scale. The height of seating must be scaled to tables and desks. End tables that are the same height as the arms of chairs and sofas will be easier to reach and visually act as space expanders,

Courtesy Armstrong, Solarian Supreme/Gilliam Furniture

This room, with its pass through to the kitchen at left, does double duty as a dining room or, as arranged here, a living room. Pieces from the owner's china collection are an integral part of the decorating scheme. (For two views of the kitchen, see pages 50 and 51).

since they seem to extend the length of the furniture.

Decorate slowly; find out what you like, what you're attracted to, and then ''feel'' each item to make sure you can really live with it. Don't jump at the first color scheme or piece of furniture that captures your fancy. Think it over, try on other ideas, and shop around some more. At the same time, trust your instincts. Go with what you really like, whether it's ''in style'' or not. That's the key to creating a beautiful, individualized space that expresses your own personal style.

Although it's usually best to minimize furnishings and accessories, ''less is more'' and ''more is more'' and ''less is less'' don't always hold true. Mementos, heirlooms, artwork, found objects, and collectibles can all be used successfully in a small room. If certain objects hold meaning for you, look for ways to incorporate them into your plan. A small space can be a jewel, designed to reflect your personality. As noted decorator Billy Baldwin, who chooses to live in a small space, says: ''Small size doesn't have to mean small style.''

Chapter Two

A CATALOG OF ALTERNATIVES AND SOLUTIONS

Flexible use of existing space is the key to multiplying your living area. The smaller your home, the more important it is to think in terms of function rather than "types" of rooms or furniture. For instance, a kitchen counter can be designed to house a pull-out desk or a drafting table; a workshop can be nestled into a converted closet; or a low shelf, at sitting height, running the length of a studio apartment, can accommodate books, a stereo, and space for working or food preparation. Twin beds positioned beneath it serve for lounging by day, sleeping by night.

Keep your space priorities in mind as you read this chapter, and be on the lookout for ways to make more out of less. If you plan to do some construction, keep looking for spots with hidden potential that could have something added or built in—the space under stairs, in closets, nooks, alcoves, wide hallways, attics, basements, and high-ceilinged rooms. Replace a wall between rooms with open shelves to expand spaces as well as provide additional storage. Installing a skylight or greenhouse window might transform a dark cranny into pleasant, yet functional, living space.

Designers agree that improving the structure of your space is more important than investing in decoration or an expensive piece of furniture. If you want to reshape your interior environment, use your floor plan to explore the possibilities, then work with a good designer to translate your ideas into reality.

Sleeping

It's one third of your life, as they say in the ads, so you might as well enjoy it. Sleeping arrangements depend a lot on whether you have a separate bedroom. If you do, you may be looking for ways to adapt that room for other purposes—an office, workroom, or sitting room—or you may simply want to make it a more pleasant environment. If the bed occupies everyday living space, you'll either want to disguise it as seating or somehow separate it from the mainstream of traffic.

Whatever your circumstances, look for ways to minimize furnishings while maximizing utility. For instance, one large night table with storage drawers may serve better than two small ones. Hang a mirror above it, and the night table can also function as a dressing table. In a studio, you might use a desk as a bedside table. A blanket chest can be used for seating as well as storage, and a bookcase or a chest of drawers can function as a room divider. Beds can be combined with sitting or working.

If you have a separate bedroom, it will feel more spacious if furniture is kept to a minimum. When a large bed is placed in the middle of a room and all but the essential accessories are eliminated or stored

out of sight, you'll create a luxurious sense of openness. If space is extremely tight, however, a large bed will look smaller if placed in a corner, an alcove, or under a window, with part of its bulk concealed by throw pillows.

For children sharing a room, twin beds arranged end to end, or perpendicular to each other around a corner create more floor space. Bunk beds are the classic solution for kids who share a small room. Those constructed of tubular steel

Minimize furnishings to maximize space. The furnishings in this bedroom consist primarily of a futon on a raised platform. Placing it in the middle of the room helps make the small space seem larger.

have a less massive look than bulky, wooden ones, but the wooden ones may contain large storage drawers.

When shopping for bedroom furniture, take a look at the variety of multifunctional modular pieces on the market. Many platform beds now feature deep drawers underneath as well as headboard bookcases. Kartell manufactures a stacking drawer system that can be adapted for use as a bed; simply stack the units up to the height and width of your mattress and use them as a base. Rolling storage drawers designed to fit under your existing bed are also available.

For studio apartment dwellers or people who want a place to put up overnight guests, there is a myriad of options. The simplest is also one of the most dramatic: two sets of stacked single mattresses and box springs placed end-to-end to fill one side of the living area. This improvised banquette runs 12 feet (3.6 meters) long, and will seat quite a few people as well as hide the bed. A single mattress and box spring, placed in a corner of the room or along a wall, accomplishes almost the same thing, with less seating and sleeping room.

Studio couches are single beds with hidden frames, so seating is raised to regular bed height. Usually covered with

Courtesy Ikea

A bunk bed (*top*) is a great space-saver in the children's room; while a sofa bed (*right*) is the ultimate furnishing for a multifunctional room.

fitted spreads and lots of pillows that help create the illusion of a couch, some have an additional mechanism that converts the couch into two beds. Daybeds are similar, the only difference being a decorative frame that includes a railing or raised barrier at the foot and head. A daybed functions as a sofa when placed against a wall and piled with pillows, but usually tends to look more like a bed than a couch.

Sofa beds and convertible ottomans come in a variety of styles, but some are more suitable for full-time use than others. Some sofa bed mattresses are so thin that you can feel the metal frame supporting the bed. After a few nights of that, the floor will begin to look inviting! If you plan to sleep in a convertible bed on a regular basis, look for a mattress at least three inches (8 centimeters) thick.

Futon frames convert from couch to bed in the blink of an eye. Lightweight and comfortable, futons are usually five to ten inches (13 to 26 centimeters) thick and are great for daily use. Arise Futon's Cloud Nine model has a 2-inch (5-centimeter) layer of high-compression, high-density foam at the core of its cotton batting layers, which makes sleep a heavenly experience.

The Murphy bed is the ultimate camouflage treatment. Thanks to a spring-operated, counter-balancing mechanism, the bed folds up flat against the wall, literally disappearing into a cabinet or closet when not in use. Continually improved since 1900, Murphy beds come in models suitable for everyday or occasional use and will accommodate twin, double, queen, and king size mattresses. They require twelve to fifteen inches (31 to 38 centimeters) of recess space with cabinetry ranging from simple bi-fold doors to complete wall systems.

© Lynn Karlin 1987

If you have high ceilings, a loft bed will utilize wasted vertical space as well as add visual interest. The space under the bed can be used for working, dining, or storage. You can also reverse the functions and sleep on floor level while using the loft for another activity. Allow about seven feet (2 meters) of head clearance for a loft that requires room to stand under, five feet (1.5 meters) for seating, and four feet (1.2 meters) for sleeping. Loft beds are usually custom-built; however, a few prefabricated models are also available. The best place to install a loft is at the narrow end of an area, where the side walls can help support it. Since heat rises, lofts should be open on both sides at the upper level for better circulation.

Another possibility is to have a waist-high wooden platform custom-built for your space, with a mattress for sitting and sleeping on top, and plenty of storage drawers underneath. Or if your living space is delineated by low "conversation group" platforms, bed units can be constructed to slide out like drawers.

If you take a guerrilla approach to decorating, you might like the simplest sleeping arrangement of all: a hammock. Strung between hooks in the corner of a room, it can act as seating in the daytime or

James R. Levin/FPG Intl.

Left: The antique custom of enclosing a bed with draperies is reborn in this modern studio apartment.
Facing page: A loft bed frees up the usually wasted space under the bed.

be taken down when not in use. Mexican hammocks, handmade in the Yucatan, are designed to be slept in—the intricate network of lightweight strings gives a lot of support without digging into you as rope hammocks tend to do. Yucatan hammocks are colorful and roomy: *El matrimonio* sleeps two comfortably. Measure your space before drilling any holes, as hammocks are usually longer than they ap-

pear, and be sure to anchor hooks securely into the wall studs, or else you will be in for a rude awakening.

Since you don't need much headroom to sleep, small, low areas can also serve well. Attics and eaves can be converted into cozy bedrooms. In an alcove, a bed can be hidden in the daytime behind a pull-down shade, curtain, or standing screen. (For a "hidden" bed in the middle of a room,

construct a frame and hang draperies of transparent muslin or net to surround the bed.)

For guests, consider all of the above options, plus the less glamorous: army cots, sleeping bags, and air mattresses. Guests need a modicum of quiet and privacy, plus access to a bathroom, but given that, extra sleeping quarters can be improvised in the dining room, living room, an alcove, or even in a wide hallway.

Eating

The dining room seems to be a casualty of the space crunch of recent years. Fewer and fewer apartments have a room devoted solely to eating. People who do have this luxury often find themselves using the room for an office or something besides dining. In one-bedroom and studio apartments, the dining area is often an L-shaped extension of the living area, adjacent to the kitchen, and must be compatible with both.

Your setup here will depend on your priorities and situation. Does your family eat dinner together every evening, or do you live alone and dine out five nights a week? Do you sometimes throw parties for twenty-five or more people? You need to decide exactly how much emphasis you want to place on dining, relative to your space.

If eating at home is an off and on thing with you, your dining area can melt unobtrusively into another area by means of a fold-down table that disappears against the wall when not in use, or a work table that gets cleared off to use for dining. On the other hand, if sharing food is a joy that deserves space in your life, a dining area can be defined within a room in various ways: with lights (candles, spot or track lights, a chande-

A fold-down table increases this small kitchen's flexibility since it can serve as both an eating and a work surface. Streamlined tractor-seat stools consume very little visual space.

lier); with a room divider (a bookcase or wall unit set in the middle of the room, or curtains or standing screens that can be pulled around the table to create intimacy); or with a large area rug.

The main thing that defines a dining area is the table. A round, pedestal-base table seats a lot of people while also creating an illusion of space. Neither the eye nor your legs are encumbered by excess furniture supports (i.e., table legs). Glass topped tables also tend to look smaller. Cantilevered chairs are good for the same reason: They don't stop the eye with their bulk, and extra legs are eliminated. Using track lights instead of a chandelier in a dining area also promotes the illusion of space.

Table options can be as varied as sleeping arrangements. There are console tables that expand with the addition of leaves. Many models now provide self-storage of extra leaves, which solves the eternal problem of what to do with them when you aren't expecting dinner guests. Some models fold up into large squares, and even feature storage for extra folding chairs. Some coffee tables are adjustable to as many as five different levels, so you can raise them up to dining height whenever the need arises. Other collapsible tables with beautiful tops are designed to be stored on the wall as "art." Although these options are most often used in entertainment situations, they still may work for you on an everyday basis if eating at home isn't a high priority. Always test collapsible, adjustable, and folding tables for sturdiness before purchasing, because they can be shaky. Also check to see how easily they can be put up and taken down, or, in the case of adjustable height tables, how easily raised from level to level.

In a studio or L-shaped space, a banquette with seating on both sides of a shared back could serve for both the dining and living areas. Deep storage bins in the base of the

Courtesy Poggenpohl

Dining and cooking areas naturally flow into one another in this small home, which makes serving and cleaning up after meals a breeze.

banquette hold rarely used items. A folding picnic table works in a very narrow area.

For entertaining, create an instant dining room in the corner of the living room, work room, bedroom, or even the front porch. When additional eating surfaces are needed, a folding table is one of the simplest solutions. Or use a table with an expanding top, either separately or placed next to a table of the same height to create one big table. Two narrow tables, normally placed side by side against a wall, can be pulled out into the room and put together to seat up to six people. Snack tables can be used singly or arranged in groups to form a dining area. In a pinch, two permanent surfaces—a desk and a large end table, for instance—can each be set for large dinner parties.

Extra seating can take the form of stools, benches, folding or stacking chairs, floor pillows, banquettes, or couches. The most important thing to remember when improvising dining arrangements is that seating must be scaled to the table height. For instance, if you use occasional chairs, which are usually lower than dining room chairs, the table must be proportionately lower as well. Of if you prefer to eat Japanese style, sitting on the floor, pillows will bring guests up to coffee table height.

Above: The "trolley table," which parks under a counter, can be rolled into the combination dining room/living room for formal dining or over to the window seat, as shown here. Arched ceiling moldings suggest an arbor and help give the kitchen its English country flavor. (See page 38 for a look at the living/dining room.)

Facing page: Until homeowners decided to tear down walls for more open space, this multipurpose kitchen was two separate tiny rooms and a hallway. The window seat at left, with the railing in place, doubles as a playpen.

Courtesy Armstrong, Solarian Supreme/Gilliam Furniture

Cooking

The needs of an efficiency kitchen are quite different from those of a kitchen used for turning out elaborate gourmet meals. Think about how you use your kitchen, as well as how you want it to function. Do you feel like you're running an obstacle course every time you fix dinner? Is traffic routed straight through your work area? Would a work island give you the extra counter and storage space you crave?

Kitchens are the most often remodelled rooms in the house, with Americans spending $17.8 billion annually on renovations and changes. Inefficient work areas, inadequate counter and cabinet space, lack of electrical outlets, poor lighting and ventilation are the most frequent problems cited by dissatisfied homeowners. But if you're stuck with a small kitchen and remodelling is out of the question, storage is one secret of success. With your priorities clearly established, storage can be organized into a streamlined system and tailored to your needs.

Base your system on the point-of-first-use principle: Anything you use often should be easy to get your hands on, while less used items don't deserve prime space. For instance, if you stir fry once a week, your cleaver, wok, and sesame oil should be within an arm's reach. If you use your food processor daily, store it on the counter. If you entertain often, your fine china, crystal, table linens, and silver should be easily accessible; whereas if you have company only a couple of times a year, your stemware could be stored on the very top shelf of the cupboard. Think about how you operate in your kitchen and what's going to be most convenient for YOU, then arrange your storage accordingly.

If your space is limited, you really can't afford to store anything you don't need. Give

Courtesy St. Louis Group/Build Inc.   Photographer: Jim Hedrich

away duplicate utensils and ones you don't use to free up valuable storage space. Do you really need twenty-five steak knives? Does that fondue pot reflect your lifestyle today? Get rid of the superfluous to make room for the essential.

Once you've weeded down your kitchen paraphernalia, take advantage of "automatic organizers" to multiply your available cabinet storage. Pull-out bins, slide-out baskets, and swing-out shelves can be easily installed with a hand drill and a screwdriver. Another option is to build narrow shelves in a U-shape along the sides and across the back of an existing cupboard for storing canned goods.

You may also be able to use freestanding components such as utensil caddies and knife blocks, as well as hanging wire baskets for storing potatoes, onions, or apples.

Right: Just about everything imaginable can be organized in pull-out bins. A cross between shelves and drawers, they keep contents out of sight yet instantly retrievable. *Facing page*: A butcher block with a handy knife rack provides an efficient work area.

Brian Leatart

There may be some wasted space that could be put to better use. If you cook a lot, wall grids are great for storing utensils and pots and pans. The simplest grid is a pegboard painted to match the kitchen, with S-hooks for hanging things. You can also make a wooden grid by nailing strips of lath to a frame. If this isn't your style, check out the variety of commercial models—grids are available in everything from high-tech stainless steel to homey colonial styles.

With minor construction, you can knock out the space between wall studs and build narrow shelves for a colorful display of canned goods (or add a door if cans aren't your idea of decoration). Packing crates have been used by many designers for kitchen storage. Mounted on the wall or stacked vertically and equipped with shelves, they make a down-to-earth statement.

If you're short on counter space, but have free space in the middle of the room, try setting up an independent work station. There are islands on casters, modular islands made of banks of stacking drawers, and built-in units that fold out to triple the workspace. Or, if you have space along a wall, a freestanding antique kitchen cabinet or Hoosier cupboard works well for preparing food as well as for storing supplies,

equipment, and cookbooks. A fold-down table (even just a shelf attached to the wall with hinges), or rolling utility cart with a butcher block top are compromise solutions for very small kitchens.

If counter space is at a real premium and there's no room even for a utility cart, use one of those cutting boards designed to fit over the sink. Sturdy pull-out breadboards are another way to extend your counter space, or you can improvise more work space by

cutting a piece of wood that fits over the top of an opened drawer. Install separate drawer slides for the board and it can be stored inside the drawer when not in use.

An uncluttered work area seems larger, so think about how often you use your small appliances in relation to the space they occupy. Since they're mounted beneath your overhead cabinets, scaled-down, under-the-shelf models of toasters, toaster-ovens, coffeemakers, can openers, and

Photographs (3): Courtesy Poggenpohl

A pull-out table multiplies kitchen work space and then disappears when not in use.

Above: Closet, cupboard, and drawer organizers come in all kinds of configurations and are one of the easiest—and cheapest—ways to maximize storage space.

Facing page: Independent kitchen work stations come in all shapes and sizes; this fold-down model also provides storage space.

microwaves free up valuable work space. Black and Decker offers a full line of space-saving small appliances, and many manufacturers also offer smaller-than-normal built-in versions of major appliances.

But maybe you'e not ready to run out and buy an under-shelf microwave or a miniature built-in dishwasher. A more homespun way to increase counter space is to take a hard look at your canisters—or whatever else is currently occupying the all-important work area. Maybe you could suspend the canisters under the cabinet, or if you use a dish drainer, get one designed to be suspended over the sink.

You'll find complete organiz-ing systems at hardware, home center, and department stores, as well as in mail-order catalogs and specialty stores. (Restaurant supply stores sell wire shelving and grids that are readily adaptable for home use.) Think about what you need, and shop around before making a major purchase.

If you're tired of your kitchen

cabinets but can't afford new ones, consider adding different hardware or painting them another color. You can create a feeling of roominess in a small kitchen with light-colored cabinets, countertops, floors, and walls. And as you know, using a minimum of furniture will also make a space look bigger, though many kitchens are so small they barely hold two people, let alone a dinette set!

If the kitchen is in plain sight of the living area (in a studio apartment, for instance), sometimes it's feasible to hang matchstick blinds or install folding doors to hide the food ''prep zone.'' When you're cooking, however, it will be on display and it needs to look good. One design technique is to match all accessories—teapot, dish towels, canisters, etc.—with the apartment's main accent color for a pulled-together, coordinated look.

Right: A red and white checkerboard motif is carried through the floor covering to the wall tiles, creating a unified, high-energy look.
Facing page: Sliding tambour doors keep small appliances out of sight when not in use, helping the kitchen look clean and uncluttered.

Designer: Ellen Terry Lerner Ltd./Photo: Bill Rothschild

Living

If your living area is limited, pare down furnishings and accessories to free up important visual space. Use strong furniture shapes for eye-catching impact, and don't be afraid to experiment with color. Look for groupings that will create a grander flow of space. For instance, in an L-shaped room, use the L for seating to lead the eye out and around. On the other hand, if your living room is large, you may want to demarcate separate areas. Modular seating extended along one side and then out into the room will "wall off" a spot, for instance. Lighting can also help divide—or unify—a space.

Built-ins, whether for storage, display, or furniture, take up less space than freestanding pieces and look sleek and trim. But if you don't have these amenities and don't care to add them, modular wall systems are a great alternative. They can be rearranged at will and taken with you when you move. Multipurpose furniture and efficient storage are two of the best ways to maximize space, and wall systems provide the best of both worlds.

Wall-to-wall storage unobtrusively "widens" a space while providing a hiding place for requisite entertainment gear. Wall systems can double

© Derrick & Love 1987

This apartment is very low on space, but the revolving storage unit, at right, helps make use of every last inch. The unit houses, among other things, the TV and stereo system.

or triple your living area, because the walls replace furniture functions and free up floor space. A custom designed system can wrap around corners, go over and under windows, and around light switches, using every inch of available wall space. With the measurements and specifications from Chapter One, you can design an arrangement to accommodate your unique situation, even allowing for the artwork you want to display. Wall systems can be used in any room, from bedroom to living room to bath. They may also function as room dividers. You'll find a fantastic selection of pieces to choose from—modular shelves, storage cabinets, roll-top and drop-leaf desks, bars, display pieces, stereo and TV cabinets, computer pieces. Some lines have more than 100 separate pieces, in more than 30 finishes and styles.

As always, when space is tight, consider furniture that does double duty such as coffee tables with deep, pull-out storage bins and low, storage units that also act as lamp tables or end tables. Similarly, floor-to-ceiling bookcases provide lots of storage in a small amount of space. Shelves can also be backed with mirrors to make the room seem larger.

So, while a glass-topped coffee table is the classic choice to keep a room from seeming cluttered, you have to weigh that look against storage options and the balance of the room as a whole. Similarly, a white laminate wall unit will blend into white walls to expand a space, but maybe you prefer natural wood. This book is intended to help you make educated decisions, not to dictate taste. Ultimately, you should go with what you really like, whether it promotes an optical illusion or not.

Courtesy Ikea

Large, open shelving provides a decorative display area for books, knickknacks, and stereo equipment. The light color of this wall unit helps it visually blend in with the rest of the interior.

Room Dividers

Room dividers define living areas, concentrate specific activities in one place, allow heat and light to flow freely, and encourage communication between rooms. They can be permanent or movable, see-through or solid, custom-built or manufactured. A platform, a small sofa, a bookcase, modular seating, and even a desk can be used as room dividers. Even tall plants, placed two or three in a row, divide a room successfully.

Folding screens are a time-honored means of breaking up space or hiding an unattractive view such as a radiator, messy shelves, or the washing machine. They can also serve to create an extra closet or wall. Usually consisting of three or more panels, screens are made of just about anything: rattan, wood, shoji, metal, leather, mirrored glass, plastic. They can also be covered in cork, felt, wallpaper, or fabric to match the room. Screens are easily tipped over, so if possible, place them next to a solid piece of furniture or near a wall, or even attach them to the wall. The screen can then be folded up against the wall when not in use.

Fixed architectural features such as alcoves serve to separate smaller areas. An area rug that extends out into the room beyond the edges of the nook makes the space seem bigger, as does hanging a large painting on the back wall. Columns and posts break up space vertically, as do the different levels created by pits and platforms.

If you opt to build a partition wall (or even if you already have one), try cutting niches at various heights between the studs of the dividing wall for displaying sculpture or pottery. This expands the visual space while improving air circulation and allowing light to spill through. For a makeshift wall, hang panels of canvas or other heavy fabric from ceiling to floor on rods and hooks. You can also use a large painting, a rug, or even a sheet of treated metal. For a see-through divider, use lightweight or casement material.

Above: This small apartment is divided by a glass brick wall, which creates privacy while allowing light to pass from one room to another. A walk-in closet is visible behind the bed.

Facing page: The other room of this apartment gracefully combines dining, casual breakfast, and living areas.

Above: The streamlined desk and high-tech lighting create an efficient, modern look in this small room.

Facing page: This desk folds neatly back into the wall unit when not in use, opening up the space for other activities.

Working

If you must integrate your work space into the main living area, look for ways to adapt "office" furniture to other purposes. For instance, use a narrow table instead of a regular size desk, so it can be pulled into service for dining, as well. Or if you have a wonderfully comfortable desk chair, buy matching chairs for dining. A file cabinet on casters can be covered with a pretty cloth and rolled over to the table to use for serving at parties.

A drop-lid work area built into a bookcase or wall unit will eliminate the need for a space-eating desk altogether. Also, a closet can be converted into a mini-office or workshop. Remove the rod and shelves, maybe even the door, then add lighting, shelves, cabinets, and a work surface and you're in business. Use the inside of closet doors for storage by installing pegboard or narrow shelves, or simply take the door off altogether.

Courtesy Techline By Marshall Erdman and Associates

Lighting

Good lighting can make any room seem larger. From the dazzling array of fixtures available, choose lighting that serves your specific purpose. Wall-mounted lamps save on space, if that's important; whereas a sculptured floor lamp or *torchère* will stake a claim in the room while making a dramatic statement. The soft wash of light provided by recessed ceiling lights or track lights can push the ceiling up and the walls out.

Background lighting provides overall visibility. It can also serve to accent furnishings and architecture. By nature, background lighting is indirect, as it's created by bouncing light off the ceiling, walls, and floor. Sources of background lighting include floor lamps, pendants, table or standard lamps, *torchères,* and bowl-shaped wall lights, as well as concealed fluorescent lighting. To get the most mileage out of the space-expanding qualities of background lighting, ceiling and walls should be of high reflectivity—white or pale painted surfaces. And they should be mat—glossy surfaces may pick up the reflected color-cast of the carpet.

Table lights are often beautiful or decorative in their own right—a Tiffany glass shade or a designer creation serves as a visual accent as well as a source of illumination. Table lamps are useful as ''punctuation.'' Their arrangement in a room also helps define various areas. Floor lamps demand more space than other fittings, but they act as subtle room dividers while providing height and visual interest.

If you wash or graze one entire wall with light it will usually make the space look larger. Both washing and grazing involve directing a row of lights toward the wall; the only difference is that in grazing, fixtures are placed a little closer to the wall. For a wash, lights are carefully angled to produce a soft, flat illumination that can be used to accentuate a book-

case or a wall of pictures, or just to provide restful background light. Grazed light is slightly stronger and more directional. It picks out textures by casting a pattern of shadows and highlights. Thus, grazed light is especially good for playing up the surface of textile hangings or brick walls. These options are feasible only if you have an expanse of wall that's uninterrupted by doors or small windows and isn't glossy or mirrored. Recessed spotlights are the best way to wash a wall with light, but renters will find track lights or a row of small portable uplights are a practical alternative.

Skylights are a great source of natural daylight. Since they're on the ceiling they automatically open up a room visually, and the light they provide will change interestingly throughout the day. Skylights let the sun shine in, and properly insulated and flashed, they'll keep out rain and heat. Some models are bubbles of plexiglass, other modular systems are designed to span 24 feet (7.3 meters) or more.

Courtesy Velux-America Inc.

Above: Skylights add visual space and drama to a room. From sunrise to sunset, the quality of light in the room is always changing.

Facing page: Skillful use of mirrors opens up this small room, which must combine dining and living areas. Precious space is saved by wall-mounting the lights.

Bathing

If you're redoing a miniscule bathroom, look for fixtures designed for corners and small spaces, including those made for boats, trailers, and laboratories. If you have a little more breathing room, consider building in a wall of storage. Some manufacturers offer modular wall systems especially designed for bathrooms. Another option is to have one custom made.

As you know, mirrors are great for lightening and brightening, or widening and lengthening a room, making its boundaries disappear. Mirrors are often given a free rein in bathrooms, and while this can be an asset to grooming, you may inadvertently multiply sins as well. If you plan to work with mirrors, refer to page 31.

Glass brick is another popular bathroom treatment. A multipurpose building material, it lets in light without sacrificing privacy. Judiciously combined with mirrors or mirrored tiles, it can drastically expand the apparent boundaries of a small bathroom.

If storage is a problem, look for wasted space that could be called into active duty. Check the walls above the toilet, tub, or at the end of a vanity; check under the sink and toilet tank, and consider ways to take advantage of the space you find. Shelves, cupboards, racks, grids, and/or pull-out bins are some of the bathroom organizers to choose from. Likewise, a mirrored medicine chest with built-in lighting is good because it serves more than one purpose. Also check out travel-sized personal appliances—not only do they take up less room, but you'll eliminate the need to store duplicates.

Courtesy Poggenpohl

Facing page: Even small bathroom spaces can be made more efficient with automatic organizers.

Left: The mirrored wall and ceiling reflect very well on this bathroom, creating a double image that tastefully omits the toilet.

Courtesy Clairson Intl.

When a wardrobe is well organized, getting dressed in the morning isn't the waking nightmare it can be if your closet is an overstuffed jumble. A closet system that incorporates a double rod allows you to store twice as many shirts, slacks, and skirts in the same space.

Storage

Closets are usually disaster zones—especially clothes closets. This is due in part to the standard pole and shelf arrangement of most closets, which wastes a lot of space, but also because we tend to accumulate too many clothes. If you haven't worn something in two years, or if it doesn't fit, it's out of date, it needs mending and you know you'll never get around to it—get rid of it!

Once you've cleared out the clutter, closet systems are the easiest way to transform your existing space into efficient storage. There are quite a few on the market, both custom-built and ready-to-assemble units; if you're handy, you can invent one yourself. Most feature a double rod so you can hang twice as many skirts, slacks, shirts, and jackets in the same space. They may also feature shelves, drawers, cubbyholes, pull-out bins, and accessory organizers like shoe, belt, and tie racks. These units can often eliminate the need for a dresser.

For narrow city closets in old houses, which often do not accommodate standard systems, you can cut wire shelves with a hacksaw and install them in the ends of the closet. Another small closet tip is to "file" everything in see-through storage boxes or sweater bags.

Courtesy Elfa Corporation

Organizing space is a continuous process. You're never really finished, because it changes as your life changes. Place things where you want them now, but don't hesitate to rearrange them when you get bored. Some people use two sets of slipcovers and drapes, switching back and forth as the seasons change. But even without such drastic measures, your home may still have different focal points at different times of the year—in December you entertain around the fireplace, in July, out on the deck. Plan your living area layout so it's flexible enough to adapt to your changing needs.

Courtesy Elfa Corporation

Stacking basket systems can be arranged in many different configurations and are adaptable to any room. They hold much more than a conventional dresser, and are a good solution for city apartments that are short on closet space.

Chapter Three

TEN CASE STUDIES

© Philip H. Ennis

By this point you've probably realized that living in a small space doesn't have to be a hardship. It can be a comfortable and rewarding experience. Now we'll take a look at ten case studies: people who have created unique environments designed to suit their individual living and working needs. Here is a family of four, a student, a songwriter, an exercise buff, and others who have addressed the limited space question with ingenuity and know-how.

As you consider the examples in this chapter, think about how you might adapt various solutions to fit your own situation. If you are an artist you may be inspired by the weaver's rooms pictured in these pages; someone with a home business may get a few ideas from the photographs of the home office and computer centers. If you like to cook you'll be interested in the kitchen photo spread.

Clearly, many design ideas are based on the jigsaw puzzle approach. Fitting all the components together is an interesting and creative challenge. When you rise above the limitations of small space living to create an environment that reflects your own personality and style, your home becomes a source of pleasure and comfort.

Bob Curtis/ Heartwood Design

E. Allen McGee/FPG Intl.

Courtesy Ikea

Architect at Home

This architect's living/working area uses a combination of natural, area, and task lighting to provide illumination for all occasions. Integrating working and living areas effectively doubles the use of the space. The drafting table helps define the conversation area, becoming an organic part of the room's layout. In addition, the low, square coffee table provides an unobtrusive anchor to that section of the room. The low wall of storage on the left makes use of otherwise wasted space in this oddly shaped room, typical of attic spaces. The storage unit consists of drawers, flat files, shelves, and an abundance of counter space.

Professor's Home Office

By concealing an office behind folding doors, this professor has the best of both worlds. Projects can be hidden out of sight when not being worked on, or expanded to fill the entire room if necessary. The window above the desk provides plenty of natural light and has the added advantage of reducing eye strain, since focusing on something faraway is the best way to rest the eyes. The entire desk unit is only about four feet (1.2 meters) deep and with the doors closed is barely noticeable.

Weaver

A loom takes up more space than many other craft accoutrements and isn't easily put away when not in use. As a result, weavers face special challenges in a small space. They also need a lot of storage for materials and supplies, often relying on a combination of shelves, baskets, and hanging storage bins. Setting up shop in a spare bedroom, an unused garage, or some other discreet space is ideal, but workshops can also be nestled into the corners of living areas.

E. Allen McGee/FPG Intl.

Gourmet Cook

Open storage in this kitchen makes everything easily accessible when it's time to get cooking. The ceiling rack holds decorative and infrequently used items; dishes and cups are stored upright near the sink for one-step storage and easy serving; and food processor blades are corralled in a special wooden bin above the counter. The rolling butcher block table adds more work space— wherever the cook decides it's needed. This floating butcher block island also features a sturdy knife rack and additional storage underneath. Assembling all ingredients beforehand and keeping utensils within an arm's reach helps make cooking in a small kitchen a pleasant experience.

Home Fitness Center

This finished basement allows for flexible use of space. Beyond the TV nook with its comfortable seating is an exercise area featuring an exercycle and a full length wall mirror with ballet bar. Unified use of wall and floor coverings and furnishings help make the home fitness center a natural extension of the living area. Note the mirrored lambrequins that make the small casement windows appear to be full length.

The corner cupboard conceals a circuit breaker box.

Diehard sports enthusiasts sometimes set aside an entire room for keeping in shape. This athlete has space to box, jump rope, lift weights, or ride the exercycle while watching the big game on TV.

Collector

Almost any collection can be displayed: stamps, butterflies, coins, and more can be framed and hung on the wall; antique furniture can be integrated into a room's floorplan; dolls, shells, and rocks can be arranged on shelves or in glass cases. A high shelf spanning the top of the room is a time-honored solution for collections of objects. This antique library card catalog is a great idea for storing audio cassettes or compact discs.

Home Computer Center

A work station that wraps around a corner provides a lot of room for writing, typing, and keyboarding. A chair on casters allows freedom of movement from one area to another, making files and storage cabinets highly accessible. The white laminate blends in with the walls, making the space seem larger, while overhead cabinets take advantage of what could be wasted space.

Designer: Allyn Kandel/Photo: Bill Rothschild

Student Room

Many students must combine study, living, and sleeping space. This can be quite a balancing act, but making the bed do double duty as a couch is one simple solution. A light-colored, wraparound wall unit combining storage with work spaces unifies the room and makes it appear larger.

© Peter Gridley 1987/FPG Intl.

Raising a Family

Bunk beds are a space-saving solution for kids who must share a small room. Open and hanging storage of books and toys makes it easy for kids to clean up after themselves. The large window allows the eye to travel up and out, making the room feel bigger.

This family created a living area by using seating to segregate a corner of their large all-purpose room. The shelf under the window and wall mounted bookcase provide decorative storage.

Courtesy Velux-America Inc.

Home Recording Studio

Designer Richard D. Lawrence and audio consultant Holly Neil created a custom home audio and recording system for this songwriter. Bi-fold doors conceal reel-to-reel tape recorders, tuner, equalizer, cassette decks, album and tape storage, while the turntable is displayed in the mirrored recess.

A custom switch panel allows the songwriter to expedite dubbing and duplicating in four directions on either tape format, and to regulate speaker control throughout the second floor.

A wall of ash cabinetry conceals the kitchen audio system; cabinet interiors are automatically illuminated when the doors are opened. The Technics Linear Tracking turntable is raised on an angle for easier operation.

SOURCES

Professional Organizations

Architectural Association
34-6 Bedford Square
London
WC1B 3ES
01-636 0974

British Decorators Association
12-15 Union House
Union Drive
Boldmere, Sutton Coldfield
B73 5TN
021 355 1068

Society of Industrial Artists and Designers
Wash House
Carlton House Terrace
London
SW1Y 5AH
01-930 1911

Manufacturers and Retailers

· **Antocks Lairn Ltd.**
Lancaster Road
Cressex
High Wycombe
HP12 3HZ
0494 24912
    London showroom:
    15 Rathbone Place
London
W1P 1AF
01-636 3248
(Stacking chairs)

· **Apollo Window Blinds Ltd.**
Johnstone Avenue
Glasgow
G52 4YH
041 883 8800
(Louvre and venetian blinds)

· **Aram Design Ltd.**
3 Kean Street
London
WC2B 4AT
01-636 6568
(Lighting)

· **Armitage Shanks Ltd.**
Armitage, Rugeley
Staffs
WS15 4BT
0543 490253
(Bathroom fixtures)

· **Artemide GB Ltd.**
17-19 Neal Street
London
WC2H 9PU
01-836 6753
(Lighting)

· **G.P. & J. Baker Ltd.**
18 Berners Street
London
W1P 4JA
01-636 8412

· **Bathroom and Shower Centre**
204 Great Portland Street
London
W1N 6AT
01-388 7631

· **Bathrooms Plus/Kitchens Plus**
19 Kensington Court Place
London
W8 5ET
01-937 5858

Cole & Son Ltd.
18 Mortimer Street
London
W1A 4BU
01-580 1066
(Wallpapers)

Crown Decorative Products Ltd.
Crown House
Hollins Road
Darwen
BB3 0BG
0254 74951
(Paints)

· **CubeStore Ltd.**
58 Pembroke Road
London
W8 6NX
01-994 6016
(Storage Systems)

· **Cubic Metre Furniture**
17-18 Great Sutton Street
London
EC1V 0DN
01-253 7557
(Adjustable shelving, office chairs, tables)

· **Czech & Speake**
39 Jermyn Street
London
SW1 9DA
01-439 0216
(Bathroom fixtures)

· **ETS Manufacturing Ltd.**
8 Pound Barton
Sutton Veny
Warminster
BA12 7AY
0985 40312
(Shower manufacturers)

· **Faber Blinds (GB) Ltd.**
Viking House
Langley Bridge Road
London
SE26 5AQ
01-659 2126
(Louvre blinds)

· **Flos Ltd.**
Heath Hall
Heath Wakefield
WF1 5SL
0924 336 4467
(Lighting)

· **Forma**
149 Upper Richmond Road
London
SW15 2TX
01-788 2538

· **The Futon Company**
654a Fulham Road
London
SW6 5PY
01-736 9190

- **Galetti**
72-6 Haverstock Hill
London
NW3 2BE
01-485 3100
(Sofa beds, beds and chairs)

- **Habitat Designs, Ltd.**
Habitat and Heals Contracts
22 Torrington Place
London
WC1E 7LH
01-636 3464

Handmade Carpets Ltd.
Sabre House
1 Shaftesbury Road
London
N18 1SS
01-803 7416
(Rugs and carpets)

- **Homecharm Furniture**
P.O. Box 33
Manchester Old Road
Manchester
M24 1AR
061 653 9191
(Fitted kitchens)

- **Ideal Standard Ltd.**
P.O. Box 60
National Avenue
Hull
HU5 4JE
0482 46461
(Bathroom fixtures)

- **Just Kitchens**
242-4 Fulham Road
London
SW10 9NA
01-352 5835

Liberty & Co.
Regent Street
London
W1R 6AH
01-734 1234
(Fabrics, carpets)

- **Lighting Centre**
676 High Road
London
N12 9PT
01-445 1765

- **Lighting Design Services**
205 Kentish Town Road
London
NW5 2JU
01-631 1424

- **Marshall Interiors Ltd.**
302 Fulham Road
London
SW10 9QH
01-351351 6838
(Paints and coatings)

- **David Mellor**
4 Sloane Square
London
SW1W 8EE
01-730 6020
(Kitchen planners and furnishers)

- **Michel & Polgar Ltd.**
41 Blandford Street
London
W1H 3AE
01-935 9629
(Unit furniture)

- **Mr. Light**
279 Kings Road
London
SW3 5EW
01-352 8398
(Lighting)

John S. Oliver Ltd.
33 Pembridge Road
London
W11 3HG
01-221 6466
(Paints and coatings)

- **Osborne & Little Ltd.**
304 Kings Road
London
SW3 5UH
01-352 1456/7/8
(Wallpapers and co-ordinating fabrics)

- **Princes Design Works**
65-75 Coburg Road
London
SE5 OHU
01-708 0502

- **Priory Furniture Ltd.**
P.O. Box 15
Saxon Works
Medlock Street
Manchester
M35 7BT
061 370 5151
(Folding tables)

- **Reylon Ltd.**
P.O. Box 1
Wellington
TA21 8NN
082347 7501
(Space-saving beds and convertible sofas)

- **Simply Sofa Beds**
130 Notting Hill Gate
London
W11 3QG
01-221 1816

- **Sitting Pretty**
131 Dawes Road
London
SW6 7ER
01-381 0049
(Bathroom fixtures)

- **The Sofa Bed Factory**
219 Tottenham Court Road
London
W1P 9AF
01-636 6001

- **Stanwells Homecare Centre**
6-8 Warwick Way
London
SW1V 1RU
01-834 1115
(Paints and coatings)

- **Storey Decorative Products**
White Cross
Lancaster
LA1 4XH
0524 65981
(Wall coverings)

- **Tekko & Salubra (UK) Ltd.**
9 Queen Street
Oldham
OL1 1RD
061 865 3362
(Wall coverings)

- **West One Bathrooms**
60 Queenstown Road
London
SW8 3RY
01-720 9333

INDEX